My Lifeprint™

Because My Life Matters

**My Plan for the Financial and Emotional
Well-being of My Loved Ones and Causes**

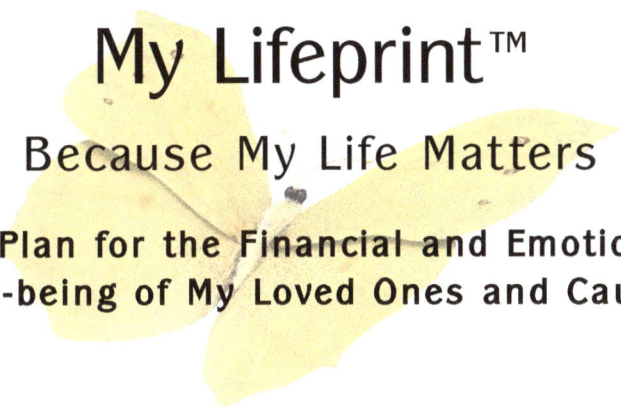

MY LIFEPRINT

Because My Life Matters

My Plan for the Financial
and Emotional Well-being of
My Loved Ones and Causes

Akua Carmichael, LLB, J.D.

Epic Press

Belleville, Ontario, Canada

My Lifeprint

Copyright © 2014, Akua Carmichael

ISBN: 978-1-4600-0197-4
LSI Edition: 978-1-4600-0198-1
E-book ISBN: 978-1-4600-0199-8
(E-book available from the Kindle Store, KOBO and the iBooks Store)

Cataloguing data available from Library and Archives Canada

To order additional copies, visit:
www.essencebookstore.com

For more information or to order additional copies, please contact:
Akua Carmichael, Barrister & Solicitor
100-400 Applewood Crescent
Vaughan, ON L4K 0C3
Tel: 416-770-4885
or www.carmichael-law.com

· *Epic Press* is an imprint of *Essence Publishing*.
For more information, contact:
20 Hanna Court, Belleville, Ontario, Canada K8P 5J2
Phone: 1-800-238-6376 • Fax: (613) 962-3055
Email: info@essence-publishing.com
Web site: www.essence-publishing.com

Printed in Canada
by
Epic
Press

DEDICATION

I dedicate this book to the memory of my father, Frank Adjei. In his last days, he told me that the one thing he would have done differently was to love more. I find these words quite significant, because my father loved many and was much loved. His lifeprint was apparent to all who were privileged to know him.

Contents

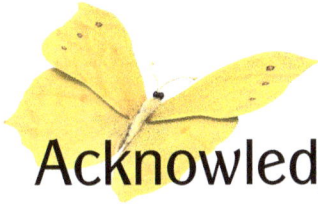

Acknowledgements

I would like to thank my great team for all their assistance in the completion of this book. It has been a dream, a long time in the making, and could not have been completed without them.

To my Lord and Saviour Jesus Christ—without you, I have no lifeprint. Thank you for the privilege to live this very life you have given me.

Thanks to Wingrove for being my greatest supporter. You are ever ready to challenge me to be all that I have been created for. Thank you. I love you.

Thanks to Josephine, Jessica, and Jada—you girls are the greatest! Your support, encouragement, and outrageous giggles make my day, every day. I love you all very much.

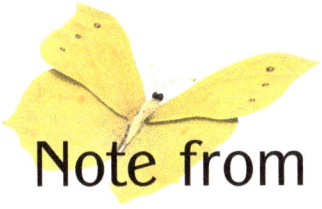

Note from the Author

As an estate planning lawyer, I have met with and spoken to hundreds of people, from various backgrounds, about the importance of having a will, powers of attorney, and other significant aspects of estate planning. I can say that just about everyone acknowledges its importance, yet so many people fail to prepare an estate plan or update it regularly once they have something in place. This phenomenon raises the question, Why?

The reasons for estate planning avoidance are varied. Some say, "I don't have the time." Others think, "I'm not rich enough." There are those who feel completely overwhelmed by the process and don't know where to start or who to call.

I've also worked with people who have difficulty thinking about and making end-of-life decisions. I can understand their concerns. Estate planning can be a highly emotional exercise—and not just for women! I've met with men, well over six feet tall and 250 pounds, who looked quite squeamish and required the support of their physically much smaller wives to get through an initial consultation.

The good news is that estate planning doesn't have to be painful. In fact, I believe it is a great opportunity to plan for the financial and emotional well-being of your loved ones and causes.

I created this manual and workbook because I feel there's a great need to educate the public about estate planning. Beyond educating, I wanted to create a book that would allow the reader to think about and record answers to important estate planning questions in preparation for meeting with an estate planning lawyer. The great thing about creating your plan is that it's uniquely yours—because no two lives or families are identical. The answers for your estate plan lie within you, waiting to be released, recorded, and implemented at the appropriate time.

You're embarking on a great journey that will have the impact of a lasting legacy. Are you ready? Get set…Go!

CHAPTER ONE

Living Life with Purpose

"The purpose of life is a life of purpose."
—Robert Byrne

This book is about estate planning and much more. Estate planning traditionally deals with the transfer of one's wealth and assets in a tax-efficient manner. I like to expand that definition to include planning for the financial and emotional well-being of loved ones and causes."

Financial Well-Being

The financial well-being of a loved one deals with planning for their financial security so that the economic loss of your passing will be manageable. You don't have to be a millionaire to adequately prepare for the financial well-being of loved ones and causes. This is where insurance professionals, financial advisors, and accountants can be very helpful. Having a solid financial plan in place is of utmost importance. We will discuss this part of estate planning in more detail in future chapters.

Emotional Well-Being

Every life impacts others and leaves a lasting legacy. Your life legacy has everything to do with the way you live your life, and fulfilling your purpose on this earth.

What kind of impact are you currently having on those closest to you? What about future generations? What will your grandchildren and great-grandchildren be saying about your life and the impact it had on their parents and grandparents? At this point you may be saying, "Now wait a minute…I'm not the CEO of a Fortune 500 company," "I don't have a big title," or "I'm just a stay-at-home mom." You may feel like no one will be saying anything about you in generations to come. You may be convinced that you have not done anything particularly significant in your life. But would you allow me disagree with you?

Do this short exercise with me. Think for a moment about your own life. What are the people in your circle saying about your parents, grandparents, or great-grandparents? Think about those who have most impacted your life. They may not be known by everyone, and their life stories may not be featured on the 6:00 p.m. news, but you and others remember them because our lives have an impact that is hopefully more positive than negative.

Don't ever think that your life and achievements are insignificant. Everyone may not hear about your accomplishments or know who you are, but there are certainly some who have heard about you and are being directly affected. They will have something to say about your life, in their lifetime and to future generations.

Think about Mother Teresa, Adolf Hitler, Martin Luther King Jr.— each one left a very distinct life legacy. The truth is, everyone leaves a life legacy. It's not optional. The only true option you have is whether you are intentional about the legacy of your life.

I have a question for you: What do you want future generations to say about you? What kind of impact do you desire your life to have? It's entirely possible to leave the life legacy you desire. You just have to be intentional about it. You must be willing to live a life of purpose on purpose. You have that opportunity right now.

This process you're embarking on is about creating your desired life legacy. Don't miss it—there are generations ahead waiting to hear and be impacted by you.

Exercises

We have considered the concept of a life legacy and the impact it can have on others. Everyone leaves a life legacy—that is not optional, but you can be intentional about the kind of impact your life has.

Answer the following questions to help you determine what kind of legacy you would like to leave. You may not have all the answers right away, and that's fine. Take some time to think about your answers, and then record them for future reference.

1) How would those closest to you describe you? (If you are unsure, conduct an informal survey.)

2) What achievement(s) are you most proud of?

---

3) What would you like to be remembered for?

4) What do you think the people closest and most important to you will say about the impact of your life on them? What would you like them to be saying?

5) Who do you think your life has most influenced to date? (Can be more than one person.) Has the impact been positive? Negative? Why?

_____

_____

_____

_____

_____

_____

_____

_____

_____

_____

_____

_____

6) What one thing can you do today to begin to impact the people you would like to?

_____

_____

_____

_____

_____

_____

_____

_____

_____

_____

_____

_____

7) What one thing can you do today to begin to change any negative or undesired impact you are currently having on others?

_____

_____

_____

_____

_____

_____

_____

_____

_____

_____

_____

_____

_____

_____

_____

_____

_____

_____

CHAPTER TWO

Your Lifeprint

"After my mother's death, I began to see her as she had really been...It was less like losing someone than discovering someone."

—Nancy Hale

Estate Planning + Life Legacy = My Lifeprint

In this chapter, I would like to introduce a term I've coined as one's *Lifeprint*. I like to think of a lifeprint as what you get when you expand the concept of estate planning to include one's life legacy. Your life legacy is the impact or mark your life leaves on others, by virtue of the way you live your life and the decisions you make throughout its duration.

Combining one's life legacy with a well thought-out and prepared estate plan results in a lifeprint. We discussed the concept of a life legacy in the preceding chapter and we will discuss estate planning in this and subsequent chapters.

Estate Planning

Estate planning is the process by which you organize your financial and personal care decision making during life and the distribution of your assets at death. A basic estate plan consists of having a will, powers of attorney, a living will, and for most people some form of insurance. The purpose of estate planning is twofold: 1) to ensure that in the event of incapacity , your financial affairs and personal care needs are being managed in your best interests, and 2) to plan for loved ones and important causes so upon your passing, your assets will be distributed to the persons and/or entities (called beneficiaries) of your choosing and your loved ones will be cared for.

Your Lifeprint

I have called a lifeprint one's plan for the financial and emotional well-being of loved ones and loved causes. Your lifeprint should include having an estate plan. It is through planning for your loved ones and causes that you can take care of their financial and emotional needs during a time of great loss. Through your will, you have the opportunity to direct how assets and monies from your estate will be managed and distributed. You can also appoint custodians and guardians for minor children to ensure they will be cared for by people you trust and approve of.

For each of us, there is a circle of people that our lives have touched and have impacted. What memories or tangibles of yourself would you like your spouse, children, friends, community groups, or others to have? Only you can answer this.

At the end of this chapter I have attached a sample ethical will, which is one option you have to pass along your knowledge and values to the next generation. Some other ways are via photos, video recordings, or perhaps a collection of family recipes or historical facts. Many people leave family heirlooms or other important pieces of personal property, including jewelry, antiques, furniture, or clothing. These items may not be particularly valuable in terms of monetary value, but they may hold great sentimental value.

The point is to consider your circle and community of loved ones and determine what you would like to leave of yourself for them. Then create or locate that thing and leave it through your estate planning documents. Your estate trustee and attorney for property (see the glossary for definition of these terms) should know of its existence. They do not have to know what it is but should know where to find it, for distribution at the appropriate time.

Let your imagination and specific goals guide you in determining what you may want to leave for your loved ones and causes.

Exercises

Your lifeprint is your plan for the financial and emotional well-being of your loved ones and loved causes. Answer the following questions to help you determine your loved ones and causes:

1) List all the people and entities you would like to leave a part (or all) of your estate to. This may include family members, friends, charities, etc.

Family members:

_____
_____
_____
_____
_____
_____
_____
_____
_____
_____

Friends:

_____
_____
_____
_____
_____
_____
_____
_____
_____
_____

Charities (churches, educational institutions, organizations, etc.):

_____
_____
_____
_____
_____
_____
_____
_____
_____

Community/Social groups:

_____
_____
_____
_____
_____
_____
_____
_____

Provision for Pets:

_____
_____
_____
_____
_____
_____
_____
_____
_____

Exercises

Personal Property Memorandum

I would like to leave the following sentimental items behind for my loved ones/entities:

Item   **Person/Entity**

_____   _____
_____   _____
_____   _____
_____   _____
_____   _____
_____   _____
_____   _____
_____   _____
_____   _____
_____   _____
_____   _____
_____   _____
_____   _____
_____   _____
_____   _____
_____   _____
_____   _____
_____   _____
_____   _____

Ethical Will (Sample)

Dear Madison,

The first time I laid eyes on you, I fell totally and completely in love. For a long time, I wasn't sure if you would even be in my life—but I'm so glad that you were. I have had so much fun being your mom. You have been a complete blessing to my life and to your father as well.

The first thing I want you know is that I love you. You are awesome, and not for all the quirky, funny, adorable things you do! No—I think you're wonderful because, even though I gave birth to you, you would never have come into existence if God had not willed it. You are here because God wanted you on this earth. I love you and I think you are awesome because God has placed a part Himself inside of you. You have been created after his image, and you are here on earth to make a significant contribution to those all around you.

You can't fail as long as you remember who you are and where you come from. You are a child of God, created after Him, and you are a partaker of the divine nature. You will do great things in your life—I know that!

There are two things I want you to do every day. In fact, if you do these two things all the time, they will become a part of your life forever. Love God, and love people. If you do these two things all the days of your life, you will be successful in every area of life. I know you can do it!

Love, Mom

CHAPTER THREE

Don't Run Out of Time

"I never lost a game. I just ran out of time."
—Bobby Layne

In this chapter we are going to continue our discussion of estate planning and the components of a well-crafted estate plan. We will also consider the relevance of time in estate planning.

I am often asked, "Do I really need a will?" Recently I spoke with someone who told me that when she thinks of estate planning she imagines a wealthy person talking about a sprawling home estate, including a guest house, several other properties, and large investment and bank accounts.

She didn't think estate planning would apply to her situation, as a woman in her late twenties in a common-law relationship, with a minor child and another one on the way. She was also in the process of building her business and had limited financial resources. However, I can say with certainty that estate planning is very important and relevant for a person in her situation.

Do you really need estate planning? Please take the following quiz and we can look at the results.

QUIZ

Circle "T" for True or "F" for False for each statement:

I am 18 years old or older.	T	F
I own property (land and/or personal goods).	T	F
I have minor children (under 18).	T	F
I will or am expecting to receive an inheritance.	T	F
I will or am expecting to receive benefits from a trust.	T	F
I am a business owner.	T	F
I am married.	T	F
I am single.	T	F
I am divorced.	T	F
I am a senior.	T	F
I am in a common-law relationship.	T	F
I have dependants (other than minor children).	T	F
I am responsible for a child/adult with special needs.	T	F

RESULTS

If you answered "T" for one or more statements, estate planning applies to your situation, and you should have an estate plan!

If you are eighteen or older, there is a high probability you answered "T" at least twice. Many will answer "T" for at least five of the statements. The quiz reveals that if you are eighteen or older you should have an estate plan.

Now, the estate planning required for an 18-year-old is not likely to be identical to the planning required at 45 years of age. Similarly, the estate planning required for a married couple is unlikely to be the same as that required for a couple in a common-law relationship. Having the right estate plan is situational; there is no "one size fits all" estate plan. It will depend on your specific life circumstance and situation.

Did it surprise you that not one statement was about your net worth or how much money you have in your bank account? If it does, that is because you are probably one of many who believe that estate planning is only for the wealthy. Not so. Estate planning is certainly for the wealthy, but it is equally if not more important for anyone who is a parent or is responsible for minor children or other dependants. Even if you do not have a high net worth, you should make arrangements through your will for the care and custody of your minor children, and provide instructions for the management of any monies you leave for them.

The "Why" of Estate Planning

It's important to understand the "why" of estate planning and the potential consequences of not having an estate plan in place. To answer the question in a general sense, not having a will and powers of attorney when an emergency or tragedy strikes will inevitably result in additional legal costs and delays that would not be present if an estate plan had previously been created and implemented. Let's look at a specific question and answer to illustrate this point:

Q: My husband and I are in our early forties, and we have three children, ages 15, 12, and 10. I'm a teacher, and my husband works in the medical industry. We own our home as well as a cottage. We live a comfortable life, although we are certainly not "rich." Neither of us has a will. What would happen if either of us (or both of us) was to pass away unexpectedly?

A: For a person who dies without a will, there are laws that dictate how assets are to be distributed. We call them *intestacy laws* because to die without a will is to die "intestate." In Ontario pursuant to the *Succession Law Reform* Act (SLRA), the first $200,000 and one-third of the deceased married spouse's estate will automatically go to the surviving spouse. The remaining two-thirds of the estate will be equally divided among the children.

In the example above, given that the children are all minors, their two-thirds share will be paid to their local court. Upon reaching age eighteen, each child will receive a one-third share. Even though the other parent is still alive, because the deceased failed to have a will prepared, giving all the assets to the surviving spouse or naming the spouse as trustee of the children's inheritance, each child's share will be held and managed by the government and not the surviving parent. When each child turns 18, the surviving parent has no authority to keep the child from receiving his or her share of the estate.

If both parents were to pass away, the issue of custody and guardianship would arise as well. In a will, parents have the opportunity to name a custodian to raise their children if they were both to pass away. Without a will, the family court decides who becomes the custodian and guardian.

Furthermore, all the assets in the deceased's estate will be frozen until someone is appointed through the court as estate trustee to manage and wind up the estate. There will be significant time delays and legal costs associated with this process that could have been avoided if both parents had implemented an estate plan.

Don't Run Out of Time

I entitled this chapter "Don't Run out of Time" because time is extremely relevant to estate planning. Most adults acknowledge they should have a will and powers of attorney or review and update existing documents.

Many cite lack of a time as the reason for not engaging in estate planning. I find that it is one of those things we keep putting off. However, life does not usually forewarn us before a disaster or an emergency strikes. Preparing your plan while you still have time is key, because at some point you will run out of time.

Common scenarios that prevent an individual from engaging in estate planning include:

- Becoming incapacitated or losing testamentary capacity— which means developing a mental or physical condition that prevents you from completing your estate planning.

- Cultural taboos and fear of death.

- Complicated family issues.

- Lack of knowledge or receiving inaccurate information about estate planning.

- Sudden death.

Given the unpredictability of life, I always encourage people to do their estate planning as soon as possible. It's not that you're expecting tragedy to strike as soon as the ink is dry from signing your will. It is simply wise to have your affairs in order and up to date.

I compare estate planning to purchasing car insurance. You would never drive without car insurance, right? When you purchase that insurance do you start thinking, "Oh no, I just bought car insurance— I think I'll have an accident really soon!"? Probably not. You more likely think, "Whew, I'm glad I got my car insurance; now I'm ready to take my car on the road! Thank goodness I have it! I won't have any worries about getting into an accident while I'm driving." In fact, getting that insurance will probably make you bolder and more confident to drive and enjoy your vehicle. So it is with estate planning. Once you have completed the process, you will likely have much peace of mind and be that much more empowered to go out and enjoy your life and loved ones to the fullest.

Exercises

My greatest concern regarding my estate planning is...

_____

_____

_____

_____

_____

_____

_____

_____

_____

I will take some time on _____ to call, or get a referral for an estate planning lawyer.

I will spend some time on _____ to start preparing for my meeting with an estate planning lawyer.

Additional notes

CHAPTER FOUR

All the Days of Your Life

"May you live all the days of your life."

—Jonathan Swift

My neighbour's house went up for sale the other week. I was surprised because my neighbour had told me she planned to live in the house she loved "forever."

By way of background, my neighbour was born in this house. Her mother died when she was very young. After graduating from high school she stayed home and looked after her father. Unfortunately, a few short years ago her father's escalating Alzheimer's proved too much and she had to move him into a full care facility.

According to the daughter, her dad had promised her she could live in the house forever and that it would belong to her when he died. She also told me that her father never got around to preparing his Will or Powers of Attorney.

I don't know why he didn't prepare these crucial documents. Perhaps he couldn't decide how best to divide his estate between the daughter who lived with and cared for him and the son he seldom saw. Perhaps he didn't think his daughter was up to assuming the role of executor and didn't know whom else to appoint. Perhaps he just never got around to it.

In the absence of a valid Power of Attorney for Property, the Public Guardian and Trustee (PGT) has taken over the father's financial affairs. The PGT gave notice to the daughter that she must move out of the house immediately so that they can sell it to raise cash to maintain the father in a nursing home.

I asked the daughter what she plans to do. She told me that, despite hav-
ing very little income, she has decided to move out of the house and rent
an apartment. She is clearly distraught over this turn of events and her
options are quite limited. She is presently considering a dependants'
claim against her father.

In some cases a failure to plan may be relatively harmless. The parent
never loses their capacity and an intestate estate distribution works out
okay. In other cases, such as this, the failure to plan (including the
preparation of Wills and Powers of Attorney and the most viable own-
ership of assets) has tragic results. The PGT is in control of the father's
finances and his devoted daughter may end up on the street.

Paul Fensom, "My Neighbour Is Moving," *All About Estates*
(blog), February 6, 2012,
http://www.allaboutestates.ca/power-of-attorney/
neighbour-moving/.

In this chapter we will be talking about powers of attorney. I like to refer to powers of attorney as the "ignored little sister" in estate planning, because many people focus only on the importance of having a will. I challenge that reasoning and would go so far as to say that having powers of attorney is equally as important as having a will.

The true story cited above highlights what can happen if powers of attorney are not prepared. One of the problems with not having an estate plan is the unintended consequences that can occur. I think it would be fair to say, based on the daughter's words, that the father intended that his daughter receive his house. It's also likely that he wanted her to be responsible for his day-to-day affairs and management of his estate while he was alive.

Failure to prepare powers of attorney cost the daughter the authority to manage her father's finances and eventually possession and possible ownership of the house that she believed was promised to her.

As we continue this discussion about powers of attorney there are some legal terms used in Ontario that I would like to define for you.

Important Terms

Continuing Power of Attorney for Property: A legal document used to appoint and grant power to an individual or institution for decision making and to manage one's financial affairs and property , even during incapacity.

Special Power of Attorney for Property: A legal document used to appoint and grant power to an individual or institution for one's financial affairs or specific property for a limited period of time.

Power of Attorney for Personal Care: A legal document used to appoint and grant power to an individual for decision making about one's personal care decisions, including health, nutrition, safety, hygiene and, shelter in the event of incapacity.

Attorney for Property: An individual or institution appointed to manage and make decisions regarding one's finances and property.

Attorney for Personal Care: An individual appointed to make personal care decisions on behalf of an incapacitated person.

Living Will: A medical care directive to the Attorney for Personal Care regarding instructions for medical treatment and end-of-life decision making. A living will can be a separate document or it can form part of the Power of Attorney for Personal Care document.

Importance of Powers of Attorney

Powers of attorney are so important because they deal with decision making for your finances and personal care while you are alive but incapacitated. When you pass away, powers of attorney are no longer effective. As of the date of death, it is the will that we look to and take instruction from.

Your choice of attorney is crucial. If you become incapacitated, you are at the mercy and care of the one whom you have appointed. It is wise to appoint a person you trust and who will act in your best interests. Typically, spouses will appoint each other as attorney for property and personal care. It's important to note that a spouse is not automatically the other's attorney by virtue of being a spouse. They must appoint each other through a power of attorney document.

Another thing to note is that you can revoke your choice of attorney for property and personal care as long as you have capacity. If at any time you lose capacity, you will no longer be able to revoke your choice of attorney. Having capacity means that you are mentally capable to make decisions about your finances and personal care.

Continuing Power of Attorney for Property

Through the continuing power of attorney for property an individual or entity is appointed to look after your financial affairs. This person or entity would be responsible for paying your bills, filing your taxes, selling your property, making investment decisions on your behalf, etc.

The power granted is extremely broad, and the only thing concerning your finances that your attorney for property cannot do is make a will for you. Great care and thought should be employed in making a choice as to whom to appoint. You are also not limited to a specific number; you can appoint one person or as many as you like. However, be forewarned that the more people you appoint, the greater the likelihood of conflict, which can lead to fighting and costly legal battles, often at the expense of the incapacitated person's estate. If you decide to name more than one person, I recommend you choose people who get along and demonstrate a history of getting along and working well together.

Your attorney for property should be trustworthy, organized, good at record-keeping, and also have the time, knowledge, and expertise to manage your finances on your behalf or work with agents who can assist. In Ontario, your attorney for property should be eighteen or older. The continuing power of attorney for property becomes effective from the date of signing, unless otherwise indicated in the document.

I am sometimes asked, "What happens if I have no spouse, children or family members to help me, or none of the relatives in my life are suitable choices? You can appoint a trusted friend or an accountant, lawyer, or corporate entity such as a trust company that will offer the service for a fee. You should also consider others who could act as alternate attorneys for property in the event that your first choice becomes incapacitated, unwilling, or unable to act. Additionally, business owners and entrepreneurs should consider having a separate continuing power of attorney for property for their business affairs.

Power of Attorney for Personal Care

Through the power of attorney for personal care, one appoints an individual who is responsible for making personal care decisions for you if you should become incapacitated. Such decisions range from where you would live upon incapacity—at home or in an assisted living facility—to what you would eat for dinner.

The power of attorney for personal care becomes effective only upon your incapacity, and in Ontario you can appoint an individual who is sixteen or older. Many of the same considerations for whom to appoint as the attorney for property apply to the appointment of the attorney for personal care. It should be someone you trust, who knows you well and will act in your best interests. This individual should be prepared to follow your wishes if you become incapacitated.

It is prudent to have a discussion with the person you are appointing as attorney for personal care about your preferences for housing, nutrition, medical treatment, and so on, beforehand, so that individual will be informed and prepared to carry out your wishes if it becomes necessary. Many wishes and preferences can be written into the power of attorney for personal care document as well.

Importance of Communication

Before appointing any person as your attorney for property or personal care, it's imperative that you discuss your desire to appoint them, to ensure they are willing to accept the appointment. No one is legally bound to accept the appointment, and can refuse to act.

Exercises

To help you in determining your best choice of attorney for property and personal care, answer the following questions:

ATTORNEY FOR PROPERTY

Who could you leave a blank cheque or credit card with and not lose a wink of sleep thinking about it? (If you have more than one person in mind, would they work well together as co-attorneys for property?)

Is this same person (or people) organized and good at record keep-
ing, documenting transactions and information? List any concerns
you may have.

ATTORNEY FOR PERSONAL CARE

Who in your life is most likely to respect and follow your requests and do what you are asking, not only when they agree with your decisions? (If you have more than one person in mind, would they work well together as co-attorneys for personal care?)

Are you a widow or widower, or do you live far away from your children or other family or close trusted friends? Perhaps your children are in your life but not a suitable choice for the task. You can consider appointing the following as your attorney for property:

1) trust company
2) lawyer
3) accountant

Given your lifestyle and personal preferences, the best choice would be:

CHAPTER FIVE

Thanks for the Memories

"Here's to the past."

—Anon.

Consider the following scenario:

June and Edmund live in Toronto and have three children—Elizabeth, age ten; Sean, age eight; and their newest arrival, Madison, one month old. June is a stay-at-home mom, while Edmund oversees and runs the family business. June and Edmund first had wills made shortly after Elizabeth was born. Time has gone by so fast! With the birth of Madison, June realizes that she and Edmund need to update their wills, as only Elizabeth is mentioned in the current ones. June puts this task on her "to do" list.

More time passes, the children continue to grow, and Madison is now two years old. In times past, June has mentioned to Edmund the importance of updating the wills—but there never seems to be enough time.

One day while Edmund is at work, June gets a call—Edmund has been in a serious accident at the manufacturing plant. June rushes to the hospital. Edmund hangs on for a few days but then passes away. June's world is turned upside down. There is so much to deal with.

The consequences of not having updated the will could be significant. Regarding the two younger kids, their share of their father's estate could be held in trust by the government until each child turns 18. Additionally, June may be forced to sell the family business to pay out the disinherited children's share if she doesn't have sufficient cash reserves.

The importance of having wills cannot be overstated. Past surveys indicate that up to 56 percent of all Canadians do not have wills. For those who do have wills, there are surveys that indicate almost half have not updated them in ten years or more. There are many benefits to having wills, including the ability to transfer your assets to the individuals and organizations of your choosing.

For parents of young children it becomes especially critical that wills are in place. Important reasons for parents of minors to have wills include naming a suitable custodian and guardian for children and ensuring that your financial assets will be managed appropriately for their benefit.

Custodian(s)/Guardian(s)

In the event that you and your spouse were to pass away together, who would you want to raise your children? In your will you have the opportunity to name a custodian and guardian. A custodian is responsible for raising your child and a guardian is responsible for managing their property and assets. You can name the same or different people to be custodian and guardian of your minor children.

In Ontario, naming a custodian and guardian in your will provides the court responsible for granting custody/guardianship of your child with a strong indication of your wishes. As parents we tend to have very strong feelings about who we would approve of to raise our children and manage their assets. Appointing a custodian and guardian through your will gives you the opportunity to let those with the power to make decisions about your child's upbringing and welfare know your desires.

Your custodian/guardian can be one or more persons. It can be a family member or friends. A custodian/guardian should be 18 years of age or older, and you should have a discussion to ensure that he or she is willing to be appointed. It is wise to also include alternate guardians, in the event your first choice is not able to act.

Testamentary Trusts

When creating your will, think about what you can leave behind for your children in terms of their financial security and well-being.

A testamentary trust is a trust that's created in your will. A trust is a legal relationship created between three parties: the settlor, the person who sets up the trust; the trustee, the person who manages and pays out the assets; and the beneficiary, the person for whom the trust is created.

Legally, your minor children cannot directly receive monies from your estate without a testamentary trust. If you and your spouse were to pass away the assets left for your minor children would be paid to the local court and held until the children turn the age of majority (18 in Ontario). At 18 their entire share would be given back to them.

Depending on the size of your estate, your 18-year-old could receive a significant amount of money. Most parents would not feel that an 18-year-old possesses the necessary maturity to manage significant financial assets. Even if that is not your concern, every time your guardian wanted or needed access to the monies held by the court, a request or formal application would have to be made, adding up to additional cost, time delays, and a long administrative process.

When you set up a trust in your will, you decide who will manage the assets on your child's behalf and the age(s) at which you want your child to receive assets and in what amount. In setting up testamentary trusts, you have an opportunity to control the financial decision making for your children until they reach an appropriate age.

Importance of Wills Beyond Custodians and Guardians and Testamentary Trusts

In addition to naming custodians and guardians and setting up testamentary trusts, wills are important because they give you an opportunity to name an estate trustee/executor. The estate trustee/executor is responsible for administering your estate, including payment of taxes and debts, and distributing your assets. It is a very time-consuming and detail-oriented job, and it requires a person who is well organized and has the requisite time.

Through your will you also have the opportunity to leave assets to friends, distant relatives, a favourite charity, or other organizations. Having a will means that you have taken the time to think about and pass on your legacy. A will is a great vehicle through which to pass on financial stability and security for surviving family members and beloved causes.

Exercises

1) If you and your spouse were to pass away at the same time, who do you feel would raise your child according to your values and in a manner most like your own? (Potential Custodian)

2) If you and your spouse were to pass away at the same time who would you trust most to prudently manage the financial assets you left behind for the benefit of your child? (Potential Guardian)

3) If you and your spouse were to pass away at the same time:

a) how would you want your child's guardian to use financial assets left behind for his/her benefit?

b) at what age(s) would you want your child to directly receive financial assets?

4) Who would you trust to act as estate trustee of your estate? Who do you feel would have the requisite time, knowledge, ability, organizational skills, and desire to carry out the required duties?

CHAPTER SIX

Assembling Your Dream Team

"Service is the rent we pay for the privilege of living on this earth."

Shirley Chisolm

There are two groups of people that can be very helpful and are indeed essential in estate planning:

1) Those who help you create your estate plan
2) Those who will carry out specific duties in the implementation of your estate plan

Create Your Estate Plan

Your estate plan will normally include a will, powers of attorney, and insurance. In creating your plan, you will have to give some thought to your financial, charitable, and other goals. Consequently, it becomes necessary to consult with your financial advisor, insurance professional, accountant, charitable giving representative, and estate planning lawyer.

You will likely require input from most, if not all, of these individuals. It is important to be aware of the role that each one plays in your estate planning.

Financial Advisor

Your financial advisor will be able to provide specific details about what financial assets you have and how they are being held, whether solely (in your name only), jointly, or with a beneficiary designation. Your financial advisor can provide information about the following types of financial assets you may own:

- Savings and chequing accounts
- Investment accounts
- Business accounts/holdings
- Registered Retired Savings Plans (RRSPs), Registered Retirement Income Funds (RIFs), pensions, annuities, and other registered accounts
- Safety deposit boxes (contents and location)

The financial advisor's role is crucial because he or she provides you with an idea of what you own and how much you would have in your estate in terms of financial assets. Many advisors can prepare and provide you with a net worth statement, which will give you an idea of the value of your estate.

Insurance Professional

Your insurance professional also plays an important role in your estate planning. This individual can provide specific information about insurance coverage and any specific insurance plans you may have in place or require.

In creating an estate plan, there are several strategies that can be implemented using insurance products to help you achieve your estate planning goals. Below is a listing of some ways insurance products are used to assist in one's estate planning:

- Registered Education Savings Plans (RESPs—providing for a child's post-secondary education.)
- Increase estate value
- Assist with tax liability issues on death
- Charitable gifts
- Business and real property concerns (ability to pass on assets without having to sell them)

Accountant

A number of tax issues arise at the time of one's passing. One of the goals of every good estate plan is to implement strategies to pass assets on in the most tax-efficient manner possible. Your accountant will play an important role in providing information about your current tax filings and history, and he or she may also provide additional information and strategies that will result in the payment of less tax upon your death.

- Tax filings (personal/business)
- Tax strategies to minimize tax liability on death

Charitable Giving Representative

Another important consideration of estate planning is charitable giving. You may want to leave a gift of cash, personal property, or land to a beloved charity or other community organization. There are favourable tax consequences that reduce the amount of tax your estate will owe if you make charitable gifts. Having a discussion with a representative of the organization you would like to leave a gift for can be helpful in completing your estate planning.

The following is a list of some of the kinds of gifts made to charities as part of an estate plan:

- RRSPs/RIFs
- Personal property (valuables)
- Real property (land)
- Insurance policy
- Stocks/securities
- Cash legacy

Estate Planning Lawyer

Your estate planning lawyer is crucial to the entire estate planning process. Ideally, your lawyer will communicate with the other advisors and representatives to ensure that all the information needed to prepare your will and powers of attorney is accurate. The estate planning lawyer is the quarterback of the entire process and should coordinate with the others to ensure the estate planning goals are achieved.

I am sometimes asked if one has to use a lawyer to draft a will. The quick answer is "no." In Ontario, you can actually prepare your own will by hand. It's called a *holograph will.* There is no legal requirement to use a lawyer. However, I do not recommend that anyone draft their will without professional assistance. Wills and other testamentary documents can be quite complicated, and it is *very* easy to leave something out or put something in that will lead to unintended consequences. I *always* advise that a person seek the professional help of a lawyer who specializes in estate planning for the drafting of their documents. It is simply a prudent thing to do.

An estate planning lawyer's duties may include the following:

- Consultation
- Document preparation: will, powers of attorney, trusts, etc.
- Discussion with other advisors

Implementation of Your Estate Plan

In your will and powers of attorney you are required to name specific individuals who will act on your behalf or carry out your wishes in the event of incapacity or death. Included in this group are

- Estate Trustee/executor and alternates
- Custodians and guardians/alternates
- Trustees for testamentary trusts/alternates
- Attorneys for property and personal care/alternates

You can name the same individual or individuals to complete all of these roles, or you can name different individuals to complete the various tasks. What is important is that you name people you believe demonstrate the requisite knowledge, expertise, ability, and time to do the job. Once you have identified these individuals, it is of utmost importance that you speak with them to ensure that they will be willing to act when the need arises.

These roles are not mandatory for the individuals you select—no one can be forced by law to act as your estate trustee, attorney for property, etc. so it is best to ensure beforehand that the individual(s) would be willing to act on your behalf.

Access to Documents

It is also important to provide access to your documents to your estate trustee, attorneys for property, guardians, etc. They should know where to locate your will, powers of attorney, and other important documents, including insurance papers, financial statements, RESP documents, etc. Your custodians should know specific details about your children that would be helpful in raising them: favourite foods, schools they attend, activities, etc. You may want to write down some of these details in a document known as a Letter of Wishes.

Exercises

Fill in the following with the names of the members of your "dream team."

CREATING YOUR ESTATE PLAN

FINANCIAL ADVISOR _____

Name: _____

Address: _____

_____

Tel/Fax: _____

Email: _____

Additional notes:

_____

_____

_____

_____

_____

_____

_____

_____

_____

_____

_____

_____

_____

_____

_____

_____

_____

_____

INSURANCE REPRESENTATIVE

Name: _____

Address: _____

_____

Tel/Fax: _____

Email: _____

Additional notes:

_____

_____

_____

_____

_____

_____

_____

_____

_____

_____

_____

_____

_____

_____

_____

_____

_____

_____

_____

_____

_____

_____

_____

ACCOUNTANT

Name: _____

Address: _____

_____

Tel/Fax: _____

Email: _____

Additional notes:

_____

_____

_____

_____

_____

_____

_____

_____

_____

_____

_____

_____

_____

_____

_____

_____

_____

_____

_____

_____

_____

_____

_____

_____

_____

_____

_____

CHARITABLE GIVING REPRESENTATIVE

Name: _____

Address: _____

Tel/Fax: _____

Email: _____

Additional notes:

_____

_____

_____

_____

_____

_____

_____

_____

_____

_____

_____

_____

_____

_____

_____

_____

_____

_____

_____

_____

_____

_____

ESTATE PLANNING LAWYER

Name: _____

Address: _____

_____

Tel/Fax: _____

Email: _____

Additional notes:

_____
_____
_____
_____
_____
_____
_____
_____
_____
_____
_____
_____
_____
_____
_____
_____
_____
_____
_____
_____
_____
_____
_____
_____

IMPLEMENTATION OF ESTATE PLAN

ESTATE TRUSTEE(S)/EXECUTOR(S)

Name: _____

Address: _____

_____

Tel/Fax: _____

Email: _____

Additional notes/Alternates:

_____

_____

_____

_____

_____

_____

_____

_____

_____

_____

_____

_____

_____

_____

_____

_____

_____

_____

_____

_____

_____

_____

_____

_____

GUARDIAN(S)

Name: _____

Address: _____

_____

Tel/Fax: _____

Email: _____

Additional notes/Alternates:

_____
_____
_____
_____
_____
_____
_____
_____
_____
_____
_____
_____
_____
_____
_____
_____
_____
_____
_____
_____
_____
_____
_____
_____
_____

CUSTODIAN(S)

Name: _____

Address: _____

_____

Tel/Fax: _____

Email: _____

Additional notes to custodians/alternates:

_____

_____

_____

_____

_____

_____

_____

_____

_____

_____

_____

_____

_____

_____

_____

_____

_____

_____

_____

_____

_____

_____

_____

_____

_____

_____

_____

TRUSTEE(S)

Name: _____

Address: _____

_____

Tel/Fax: _____

Email: _____

Additional notes/alternates:

_____
_____
_____
_____
_____
_____
_____
_____
_____
_____
_____
_____
_____
_____
_____
_____
_____
_____
_____
_____
_____
_____
_____
_____
_____
_____

ATTORNEY FOR PROPERTY

Name: _____

Address: _____

_____

Tel/Fax: _____

Email: _____

Additional notes/alternates:

_____

_____

_____

_____

_____

_____

_____

_____

_____

_____

_____

_____

_____

_____

_____

_____

_____

_____

_____

_____

_____

_____

_____

ATTORNEY FOR PERSONAL CARE

Name: _____

Address: _____

_____

Tel/Fax: _____

Email: _____

Additional notes/alternates:

_____

_____

_____

_____

_____

_____

_____

_____

_____

_____

_____

_____

_____

_____

_____

_____

_____

_____

_____

_____

_____

_____

_____

CHAPTER SEVEN

Get Started!

> "Even if you're on the right track, you'll get run over if you just sit there."
>
> —Will Rogers

Congratulations! You have come to the end of this book.

Completing your estate plan is very similar to taking care of a baby. Neither is self-sustaining! You are the key that unlocks completion of the process. The following is a list of things to do to get started with your estate planning:

1) REVIEW YOUR CURRENT ESTATE PLAN

- Do you have a will and powers of attorney? If they are more than three years old, review the documents to ensure they reflect the reality of your current situation.
- Do you want to make changes to your beneficiaries; including or deleting any?
- Do you have insurance? Your loved ones may need quick access to funds at the time of your death and insurance proceeds can be a great help.
- Ensure registered accounts (RRSP/RRIF, etc.), joint account holders, and beneficiary designations are correct and up to date.
- If you do not currently have a will and powers of attorney, read on and make plans to have the documents drawn up.

Notes:

2) TALK TO THE PEOPLE ON YOUR "DREAM TEAM"

- Decide on an estate trustee/executor, attorney for personal care, attorney for property, custodian/guardian, trustee, alternates, etc. Speak with each person and alternate to ensure they are willing to be appointed.

Notes:

3) DO A SEARCH FOR ALL YOUR IMPORTANT PAPERS, AND GATHER THEM INTO ONE PLACE

- Prepare a binder/notebook with your will, powers of attorney; insurance documents; special instructions to your custodian and guardian, trustee, etc.; financial account documents; personal property ownership documents/appraisals; charitable giving information; names and contact information of your advisors: accountant, lawyer, financial advisor, etc.; funeral information; etc.

Notes:

4) PREPARE A PERSONAL PROPERTY MEMORANDUM

- Who would you like to leave personal items including jewelry, photos, clothing, antiques, etc. to? What are the items?

Notes:

5) THINK ABOUT YOUR LIFEPRINT

- Ethical will
- Personal property memorandum
- Your life legacy

Notes:

6) DISCUSS PERSONAL CARE DECISIONS AND PREFERENCES WITH SPOUSE/PARTNER AND APPROPRIATE FAMILY MEMBERS

- Provide a list of your preferences for health care, shelter, nutrition, hygiene, safety, etc.

Notes:

7) MAKE PREPARATIONS FOR PETS

Notes:

8) CONSIDER THE BENEFITS OF SETTING UP TRUSTS IN YOUR WILL

- If you have dependants, including children, parents, special needs family members

Notes:

9) DETERMINE THE NET VALUE OF YOUR ESTATE UPON DEATH

- Calculate the total value of your assets minus your debts (including tax liability on death)

Notes:

_____

_____

_____

_____

_____

_____

_____

_____

_____

_____

_____

_____

_____

_____

_____

_____

_____

_____

_____

_____

_____

_____

_____

_____

_____

_____

_____

10) SET A DATE TO CALL/VISIT AN ESTATE PLANNING LAWYER TO GET THE PROCESS STARTED

- If you are unsure of who to call, contact your local law society (in Ontario, Law Society of Upper Canada) or ask for a referral from your friends, financial advisor, insurance agent, etc.

Notes:

Your Lifeprint Notes:

Your Lifeprint Notes:

Your Lifeprint Notes:

Glossary

Attorney for Personal Care: An individual appointed in a Power of Attorney for Personal Care, to make personal care and medical decisions on behalf of the individual appointing him/her.

Attorney for Property: An individual appointed in a Continuing Power of Attorney for Property, to make financial decisions on behalf of the individual appointing him/her.

Beneficiary: An individual or entity that receives a gift/assets from one's estate.

Bequest: A gift made to another through a will.

Continuing Power of Attorney for Property: A legal document through which an individual is appointed to have financial decision-making power for another person (usually an incapacitated individual).

Custodian: An individual appointed in one's will to have custody of a minor and to be responsible for the upbringing of that minor.

Dependant: An individual that one has a legal responsibility to care for.

Estate: All the assets and debts owned by an individual.

Estate Trustee/Executor: A person named in one's will who is responsible for the administration of one's estate, including paying debts and taxes and distributing the estate's assets to the deceased's beneficiary(ies).

Guardian: A person/persons appointed in one's will to be responsible for the management of a minor's assets.

Holograph Will: A will written entirely in one's own handwriting.

Intestacy: Occurs when a person passes away without creating a will.

Jointly/Jointly and Severally: Terms that may be found in a Power of Attorney. "Jointly" indicates that when two or more person/entities are appointed as attorneys, they must make all decisions together, and approval is required from all the attorneys to be effective. "Jointly and Severally" indicates that attorneys can make decisions jointly or independently, and those decisions must be honoured by all the attorneys.

Living Will: A health care directive through which one can express desires regarding end-of-life treatment and medical care decisions.

Personal Property: Personal and household effects and ornaments, including jewelry, cars, antiques, tools, clothing, etc.

Power of Attorney for Personal Care: A legal document through which an individual is appointed to make personal care and medical decisions on behalf of an incapacitated person.

Probate: The court process by which a will is approved as the final last will of a deceased person. The current legal term for probate in Ontario is the "Application for a Certificate of Appointment of Estate Trustee with a Will."

Real Property: Refers to land, buildings, real estate.

Residue: That portion of one's estate that remains after specific gifts, bequests, have been made.

Trustee: A person or entity responsible for distributing the assets in a trust (trust property) and for managing the trust. The Trustee holds legal title to the trust assets.

Trusts (Testamentary, Inter Vivos): A trust is a legal arrangement between a Settlor (the person setting up the trust), a Trustee (a person or institution holding legal title to trust property and responsible for distributing the property per the Settlor's instructions), and the Beneficiary (the person/entity that receives or benefits from the trust property). Trusts are called *inter vivos* when they are created during the lifetime of the Settlor. A testamentary trust is created in the will of the Settlor and takes effect upon the death of the Settlor.

Will: A legal document through which a person can distribute assets of death.

www.ingramcontent.com/pod-product-compliance
Lightning Source LLC
Chambersburg PA
CBHW070410200326
41518CB00011B/2141